Catfish

Bottom-Dwellers

Dr. Richard A. NeSmith

Love of Nature Series

ISSUE 31

Applied **P**rinciples of **E**ducation & Learning

APE-Learning *Publications*

© **2021 Richard A. NeSmith**
Love of Nature Series

JUNE 2025

ISBN: 9798702159751

FLESCH-KINCAID GRADE LEVEL: 8.8

Catfish: Bottom-Dwellers
(Class Osteichthyes)

Catfish are **bony fish** from the class **Osteichthyes**, in which *osteo-* refers to **bone** and *-itchyes* means fish. The term refers to the presence of bone in the skeleton. In comparison, shark skeletons are made of cartilage, but those of fish are of bone. Sharks, then, are from the class **Chondrichthyes**, for *chon-* refers to **cartilage**. I genuinely love this word. It may be one of my favorite science words. It is phonetically pronounced aa·stee·**ik**·thee·eez. Practice

saying it, usually stating it gets the attention of others.

As we get the terminology out of the way, we need to know one more identification term. Fish are classified into three

Blue catfish

groups.[1] Catfish are **ray-finned** fish called **teleost,** meaning

Blue catfish.

complete boned, which make up 96 percent of all fish. Having ray-fins means that their fins are *webs of skin*. Those fins are supported by a bony substance similar to that same substance a cow's horn is made, instead of the fleshy, lobed fins on other types of fish. For the most part, *catfish are bottom-dwellers*.

Range

Catfish can live and even thrive in temperatures from just above freezing to nearly 100 degrees Fahrenheit. If there is enough water, there is probably fish.[2] Though over-fishing by some commercial enterprises has almost eliminated the fish from some environments, most bodies of water still have fish.[3]

Though all fish live in water, not all fish can live in the

---

[1] Agnatha (jawless fishes), class Chondrichthyes (cartilaginous fishes), and superclass Osteichthyes (bony fishes).
[2] A pond that forms near other ponds may receive new fish from passing birds of prey dropping their catch. Similarly, fish roe (eggs) that remains damp enough during a trip between ponds may wash off of the fur and feet of local animals as they move from pond to pond.
[3] The Sargasso Sea. See: https://oceanservice.noaa.gov/facts/sargassosea.html

same kinds of water. Catfish species today live inland or in the coastal waters of every continent *except* Antarctica. They are most diverse in tropical South America, Asia, and Africa, with one family native to North America and one family in Europe.

To better understand catfish, it will be useful to consider what Osteichthyes are and what characteristics they share.

Introduction to Osteichthyes

Osteichthyes includes more than 28,000 **species** and is the largest number of living species of all scientific classes of **vertebrates**. This class consists of all bony fishes. Yes, in science, the plural of "fish" is *fishes*. However, English permits the word *fish* to be singular or plural.

All Osteichthyes are cold-blooded vertebrates that breathe through gills and use fins for swimming. Bony fishes share six distinguishing characteristics:

1. skeleton of bone
2. scales
3. paired fins
4. one pair of gill openings
5. jaws
6. paired nostrils

Bony fish make up 96% of all fish species.[4] Catfish are found in one of three subclasses.[5] A **fish biologist** is called an **ichthyologist**, and today they recognize over 500 different bony fish families. That is a lot of *fish-n-chips*! And that's not entirely a bad thing since currently, 3.2 *billion* people rely on fish for almost 20 percent of their animal

---

[4] Fishes not included in the Osteichthyes are the Chondrichthyes (sharks and their relatives), the Myxini (hagfishes), and the Cephalaspidomorphi (lampreys).
[5] Three subclasses of Osteichthyes include Dipnoi, Crossopterygii, and Actinopterygii.

protein intake.

About 75 percent of the world's fish catch is used for human consumption. The remainder is converted into fish-meal and oil, primarily for animal feed (including farmed fish). Finally, fish are significant to us for ten percent of the world's population depends on fisheries for their livelihoods.

In the United States, the average American consumes 16.1 pounds (lbs.) of seafood per year.[6] Catfish seem to be ranked in the top seven favorite species of fish to eat. There are some concerns about consuming bottom-feeders. They could be eating **toxins** and parts of dead fish that eventually settle on the lake, river, or ocean bottom. However, the confusion lies in that *most catfish are bottom dwellers*, but not all catfish are entirely bottom feeders. Flatheads, for example, rarely feed on dead (**carrion**) or

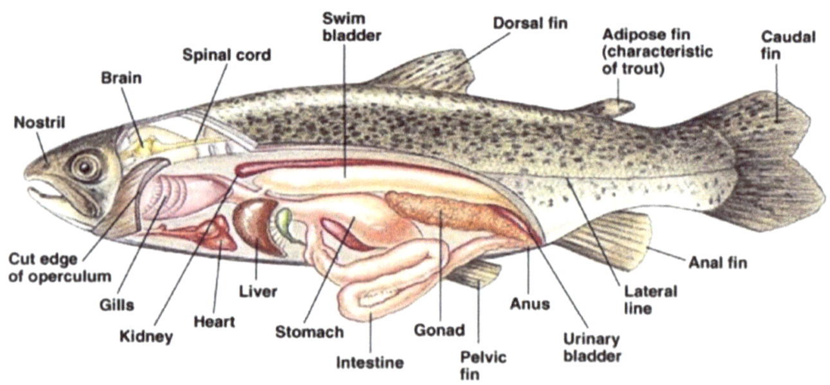

decaying matter. Despite warnings about eating any fish containing possible high concentrations of contaminants

Anatomy of Bony Fish.

---

[6] According to the latest "Fisheries of the United States" report released by NOAA Fisheries

such as lead, mercury, PCBs, and dioxins,[7] catfish make a delicious food dish. The FDA has placed it in the "Best Choices" for fish consumption.

Characteristics

Adult catfish are usually solitary creatures and can be of various colors depending on the environment in which they

live. Common colors include olive, light blue, and bluish-gray.

Brown Bullhead (Ameiurus nebulosus)

All catfish live in water. Not all fish, however, can live in the same quality of water. Fish can tolerate different environmental conditions. We will address some of these conditions. Such ecological factors require adaptations for

---

[7] US Food and Drug Commission recommend no more than two or three servings per week. See: https://www.fda.gov/food/consumers/advice-about-eating-fish

survival. Six such factors include the:

1. Amounts of salt (salinity)
2. Amounts of oxygen (diffused O_2)
3. Types and availability of food
4. Water temperature
5. Hiding areas (cover and the bottom)
6. Breeding areas

Salinity

You may have noticed that some fish live in freshwater only, while others are exclusively saltwater. Those on the verge live in freshwater and venture in saltwater for short periods or live in saltwater and occasionally venture in freshwater. Finally, those fish live in brackish waters, which have a salt (*saline*) content but much less than oceans and seas. One major factor that separates fish is **salt**. Some fish cannot live in areas where there is much salt, and others need salt in the water to live. However, some fish can live in both saltwater and freshwater!

Black Bullhead.

There is a reason for such a restriction. It's called *osmoregulation*, and it has to do with water movement inside or outside of the body. The technical side maintains constant osmotic pressure in an organism's fluids by controlling water and salt concentrations. Natural biological salts include **sodium chloride** and other minor salt compounds.

The body seeks to maintain a **dynamic equilibrium**, which means a healthy balance. Water moving into a cell is offset by water moving out of that cell. The goal is to become and maintain a state of being **isotonic** (equal on both sides of a cell membrane). This natural water movement (called **osmosis**) means that a fish living in saltwater would naturally *lose body fluids* escaping due to the outer environment having a higher salt concentration than inside their body. This results in **dehydration** and death.

A fish living in freshwater will naturally gain excessive

water inside their body as the salt concentration is greater

Hardhead Catfish (Noturus insignis).

Stonecat Madtom (Noturus flavus).

than in the water in which they live. **Osmosis** results in the body swelling until death occurred.

A **marine** (saltwater) fish has an internal osmotic concentration lower than that of the surrounding seawater, so it tends to lose water (to the more negative surroundings), increasing the salt concentration.[8] In freshwater, the inside of a fish's body has a higher salt concentration than the external environment. Consequently, there is a tendency to lose salt and absorb water. To combat this, freshwater fish have very efficient **kidneys** that **excrete** *water quickly.*[9]

The determining factor of whether a fish is freshwater, saltwater, or brackish water is based on the kidneys' ability in each species. The kidneys monitor and regulate the body's saline content.

---

[8] Saltwater fish cannot stop water from diffusing into them, so prolonged exposure to less than 1.008 will kill them.

[9] In comparison, the human body contains many salts, of which sodium chloride is the major one, making up around 0.4 percent of the body's weight at a concentration pretty well equivalent to that in seawater.

Freshwater

Freshwater contains much less salt than the ocean.[10] Most ponds, streams, rivers, and reservoirs across North America are freshwater. Some common freshwater fish are bluegills, carp, crappie, bass, perch, northern pike, trout, walleye, and **catfish.**

In North America, freshwater catfish called **ictalurids** (literally interpreted as *fish cats*) includes about 51 species. Common names include madtoms, channel catfish, blue catfish, and bullheads. Bullheads are the largest and most known. Though some of these catfish have been introduced to habitats they are not native to (thus becoming invasive species to those regions), sports fishers seem to complain little about their impact due to the return

---

[10] Fresh water has a salinity of 0.5 ppt (parts per thousand) or less. Seawater is about 35 parts per thousand.

they gain.[11]

Saltwater

Many kinds of fish live in the salty water of the oceans. A fish's kidney keeps the proper balance of salt in its body. These fish had adapted ways in which their kidneys can

Slender madtom (Noturus *exili*)

pump out the extra salt while keeping their water levels in balance.

Popular saltwater fish include bluefish, cod, flounder, striped bass[12], sea trout, tarpon, tuna, halibut, rockfish, sea perch, lingcod, yellowtail, and yes, even *catfish*. This includes **Gafftopsail catfish** and the **hardhead catfish**.

Brackish Water

---

[11] This is not uncommon of animals important to sports hunting enthusiasts, as can also be seen in the invasive wild hog population taking over and destroying many forests in North America. See: *Love of Nature*: Issue 23: *Wild Hogs and Peccaries: Disruptive Invaders*.

[12] These also found in freshwater.

The term **_brackish_** is an old German word meaning salty. Brackish water is water with salinity levels between seawater and freshwater. These occur where surface or

groundwater mixes with seawater, often in deep **fossil aquifers**, or salt dissolves from mineral deposits over time as rain penetrates aquifers. Also, estuaries are often freshwater, where streams and rivers meet the saltwater ocean. In these environments, the salinity changes daily with the tide's ebb and flow, with rains, and during drought times.

The amount of salinity determines the types of fish that live in estuaries. Generally, the species found in these waters include redfish, sea trout, snook, striped bass, and the two types of saltwater catfish. Some fish live in saltwater but

Flathead catfish (Pylodictis olivaris)

swim up rivers and streams to lay their eggs (**spawn**).[13] They include shad, salmon, and some types of trout.

Blue catfish.

Estuaries are essential **biomes** to the **ecosystem**. They are nurseries for so many other animals, including some of the deep-sea oceanic fish. If an estuary becomes polluted, it endangers all.

Oxygen

All *aerobic* animals require oxygen (O_2) intake and the exchange (removal) of carbon dioxide (CO_2) in the metabolic process. This is referred to as ***respiration,*** and some accomplish this with lungs. Fish, typically, breathe

---

[13] These types of fish are referred to as anadromous fish, from the stems, *ana-* meaning "up" and *-dromos* meaning "running."

through gills, though some can do so through the skin (***cutaneous respiration***).[14] In some catfish species, a **mucus** layer covers the skin and can be used in the

---

[14] Some species of catfish are able to breathe through their skin, which is why most species of catfish are lacking scales and have smooth, mucus covered skin.

Catfish are preyed upon by bass and other fish.

oxygen-carbon dioxide exchange. **Scales** are one of the characteristics of Osteichthyes. However, we will find that catfish violate this rule. There is little explanation in the scientific literature as to why this is so. Catfish do not have scales, and their bodies are said to be naked.[15] In some catfish, the skin is covered in bony plates called **scutes**; some form of body armor appears in various ways within the order.

Sometimes, however, when diffused oxygen levels are low, fish will surface and *gulp* the atmospheric air. The low oxygen levels are mainly due to a lack of aeration, poor water quality, or water that has become too warm (all of which reduce dissolved oxygen levels). These can cause the fish to become stressed. During such times of stress, fish can act or swim strangely.

---

[15] Unlike most other fish, catfish are scaleless, distinguishing them from most other ray-finned fishes (teleost).

Some fish require more **oxygen** than others. Living plants in lakes or streams add oxygen to the water through **photosynthesis**. One may remember that photosynthesis takes in sunlight energy and converts it to glucose by

absorbing carbon dioxide and producing oxygen as a waste product. As these water plants release oxygen, it diffuses into and saturates the water. The fish's gills extract this diffused oxygen.

Oxygen also enters the water from the environment, and even during times of rain.[16] Even the tumbling of water over rocks and rapids increases oxygen from the air. Some water environments have higher O_2 content than others, directly regulating which species of fish live there.

Oxygen levels, usually described as **dissolved oxygen**

---

[16] Rainwater (usually) a clean and natural water source is a helpful source of the dissolved oxygen for ponds, lakes, and rivers.

(DO), are always changing, not only seasonally but daily (from night to day), and even hourly, based on temperature. Water temperature can vary at different locations in the lake or ocean. Colder water holds higher O_2 contents than warmer water. This also means that as one travels down the **thermocline**[17] in a lake or ocean, the temperature decreases due to reduced sunlight and the level of oxygen available for fish respiration. Decaying plants reduce oxygen during decay. Pollution and various chemicals also reduce dissolved oxygen in the water and can cause *fish kills*.

Some fish can live in a wide range of temperatures, but some, like trout, require cold water.[18] Although fish cannot always find the exact temperature they prefer, they are usually found in waters close to that temperature. Each fish

---

[17] The thermocline is a steep temperature gradient in a body of water such as a lake. The water is at different temperatures marked by a layer above and below, which prevents mixing between the surface waters and that beneath the thermocline.
[18] Trout may be less tolerant because of their preference to 40-45 degree clean water.

has a different range of water temperature in which it can survive.

Some birds of prey are great hunters of fish, including osprey. Also, herons, cormorants and kingfishers and even the fish-eating owl!

As many public utility companies currently practice, the industrial heating of water alters the environment and reduces fish populations and the amount of oxygen molecules the water can hold.

Food

Food availability is another factor that is essential in how well fish occupy a water habitat. This is also affected by the amount of *competition* with other fish. Such factors include standing crops (number *and* weight of fish in the habitat), fish size, water temperature, water quality, and weather.

Water Quality

Water quality affects fish species differently. Some fish are more tolerant of poor water quality. Some are not. Some catfish prefer stagnant water, and others are limited to rivers and streams with fast-moving currents. Some catfish species are **nocturnal** (sleeping during the day), while others are **diurnal** (active during the day). Typically, nocturnal catfish hide under rocks and leafy debris or bury themselves in the mud during the day. Some fishermen report that night fishing is better in the summer mainly because catfish move from deeper water to shallows to feed at night, making them easier to find and catch.

However, water that is stagnant, polluted, or lacking adequate oxygen will not support large numbers of fish.

Chemical toxins or other human-produced pollution can be detrimental. Currently, 100 million marine animals die each year from plastic waste alone. Not all fish can tolerate pollution (like trout), but some (like carp) are more tolerant.

Most catfish species prefer clean, well-oxygenated waters and can be found living in ponds and reservoirs. They do, however, tolerate muddy water and seem to actually like mud.

Oxygen is vital. Food is important. And, clean water is essential. But, finally, fish must also have *coverage*. Cover includes aquatic plants and grasses, logs, rocks, and some means of hiding themselves and their eggs. Coverage provides fish with protection from their predators. It also enables them to prey on unexpecting fish.

Recognizing the environmental factors that fish encounter, the biological needs to survive are critical as we consider

catfish. Catfish are named based on their catlike whisker feelers (called **barbels**) on each side of the mouth. These are **sensory organs** located on the nose and the chin and are vital adaptations for their survival.

Also, catfish have **chemoreceptors** across their entire bodies. This means they *taste* anything they touch and feel and *smell* any chemicals in the water. It has been estimated

In murky water one can see a male catfish guarding the ball of almost transparent gelatinous mass of eggs in the nest.

that with these receptors, catfish have the equivalence of 100,000 taste buds. So, the sense of taste (**gustation**) plays a primary role in food orientation and catfish location.

Spines on the back (**dorsal**) and **pectoral** (on the chest) fins are characteristics of most catfish and act as a defense mechanism. These are as sharp as a knife, and some contain toxins.

It is a myth that catfish sting. However, their fin spines do contain a mild venom with a sting comparable to that of a honey bee. Catfish venom glands are found alongside sharp, bony spines on the dorsal and pectoral fins' edges. When threatened, these spines lock into place and become sharp knife-like defenses. When a spine jabs a potential predator, the venom gland cells' membrane is torn, releasing venom into the wound. If these spines puncture the skin, this venom causes edema (swelling) and a hemolytic (causes increased blood flow in the injury area) effect. It is the smaller catfish that most often hurt (stab) people as they grab the fish.

As the catfish eggs hatch, they stay huddled in a darkened mass for several days. The mother catfish will bring algae and drop it in the midst for dinner

The use of venom is strictly defensive and aims to deter a predator. Toxic catfish in North America have relatively mild venom. And, not all have venom, such as the popular flathead catfish.

Diet

Catfish are **bottom-dwellers**, but that does not mean they

get all their food from the bottom. A **bottom feeder** is an aquatic animal that feeds on or near the bottom of a body of water. This category includes fish such as flatfish (halibut, flounder, plaice, sole), eels, cod, haddock, bass, grouper, carp, bream (snapper), and some species of shark. One thing is sure, catfish love to eat. Catfish play a vital role in the **food web**, preying on and becoming prey.

Catfish travel to where the food is, whether it means cruising along on a riverbed or browsing the water's surface looking for larger prey. Wild catfish have very diverse

Within a few weeks, catfish hatchlings, called fries, begin feeding themselves in large shoals.

feeding behaviors. Some are more strict scavengers, while

others prefer to swallow large fish and other prey whole.

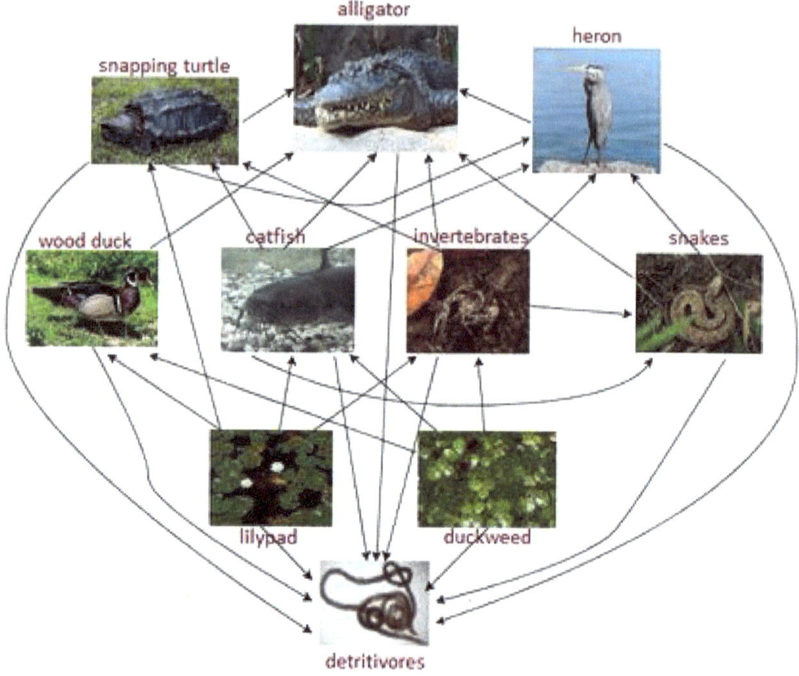

Example of a simple food web. Arrows point towards "what is doing the eating." Example: the catfish *is being eaten* by the alligator.

Catfish are, typically, opportunistic **omnivores** and feed

mostly at night. Some catfish can be **carnivores**, **herbivores**, **omnivores**, or even **limnivores** (eating microorganisms within the mud). A few select species of catfish even like to eat things like wood and algae.[19] Feeding habits depend on various factors such as weather, season, and time of day. Catfish tend to feed from sundown until midnight, but they do bite year-round.[20]

---

[19] And though none of these are in North America, there are some that are parasitic and live off the blood of other fish, frogs, rodents, and even aquatic birds.

[20] Some have shared that the best bait for catching catfish includes nightcrawlers, chicken liver, grasshoppers, minnows, cut bait, stink bait, cheese, hot dogs, and even bubble gum.

During pre-**spawn** (release or deposit of eggs), catfish feed aggressively.

Michael Gardner

A catfish's diet changes as it grows. Juvenile catfish eat small invertebrates and insect larvae. A catfish's diet changes as they grow older. Adults feed on snails, insects,

Cindy Mixon

crustaceans, crawfish, algae, plants, fish, and fish eggs. If it doesn't eat them, then they will try to eat it. They have an excellent sense of smell and are attracted to the prey with the strongest scent. Catfish are not picky. Any fish that they can reasonably swallow, will eat along with other available food sources. Any well-prepared live bait or even cut/dead fish bait will work for catching even trophy-size catfish.

Though catfish do prefer clear, clean water, they love the mud. But, mud clouds and limits light, making it difficult for fish to see prey or predators. To see under low light levels in murky water, some fish have enhanced modified eyes, including more roundish lenses.[21] Fish naturally adjust their visual *focus* by moving the lens closer to or further

from the **retina.**

Marine catfish named the Gafftopsail catfish (Bagre marinus).

---

[21] In addition, catfish use a special muscle which changes the distance of the lens from the retina. In bony fishes the muscle is called the retractor lentis, and is relaxed for near vision. Bony fishes accommodate for distance vision by moving the lens closer to the retina. In addition, some catfish family have a modified iris called an omega iris. Its function is not entirely understood at this time.

Catfish utilize their **lucidum tapetum**, a reflective layer, to view through the dark water. This creates **eyeshine** in some fish species. In the catfish's eye is a layer of protein crystals known as **guanine**, an **amino acid**, behind the fish's **retina**. The guanine in the back of the retina reflects light through the retina, increasing the amount of light that reaches the **rods** and **cone** receptors in the eye.

Cone cells provide catfish with color vision, but this is not very useful as they are of little use in dark or murky water. **Rod cells**, however, are highly sensitive to low light providing **night vision**.[22] This possibly makes vision more enhanced for catfish at night. Eyeshine allows fish to see well in low-light conditions and **turbid** (stained, or rough, breaking) waters, giving them an advantage over their prey. This enhanced vision allows fish to populate the deeper regions in the ocean or a lake.[23]

---

[22] Some fish can even see ultraviolet light and some are sensitive to polarized light.

[23] An extremely rare eyeless catfish species previously known to exist only in Mexico has been discovered in Texas. See: http://bit.ly/3r327ns

Behaviors

Like any other animal, fish species have a set of instinctive behaviors that generally remain consistent during normal and healthy periods. These can include various survival strategies, whether mating, communicating, or merely regulating their body temperature.

Communication

Catfish are a few fishes that can communicate with other fish underwater through an organ called the **Weberian apparatus** or **ossicles** (a chain of four pairs of tiny bones similar to that in the human eardrum). However, the fish does not have external ear openings. These bones are

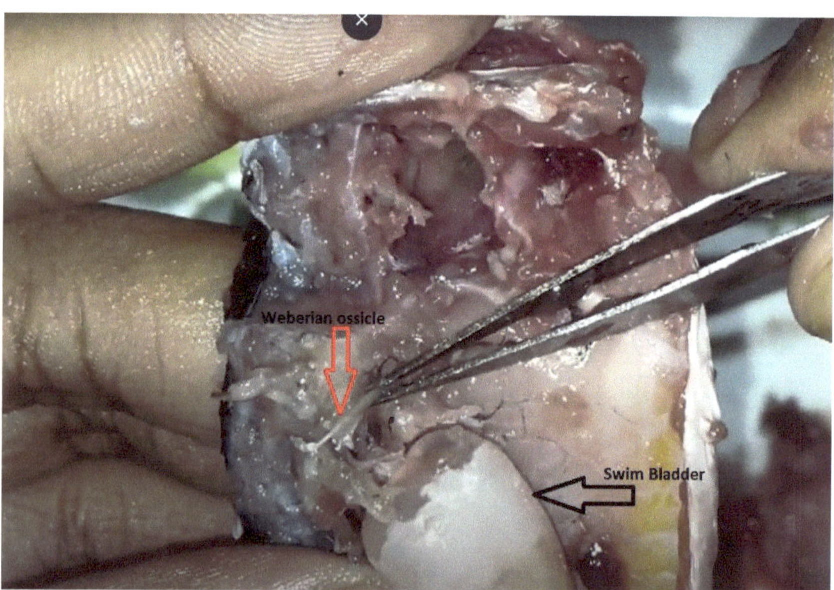

located on each side of the fish behind the gills and before the swim bladder. They grow internally to *physically connect* the auditory system becoming a simple inner ear connected to the **swim bladder**.

In practical terms, these bones/ossicles receive sounds. It transmits what sometimes resembles a clicking or faint plucking sound of strings or rattling sounds. This bodily structure improves hearing and communication by *amplifying sound* and enabling sound production. Sound is accomplished by rubbing these ossicles together underwater. The linking to the swim bladder amplifies the sound, similar to what a drum would do when hit.[24] This apparatus intensifies the sound waves that would otherwise

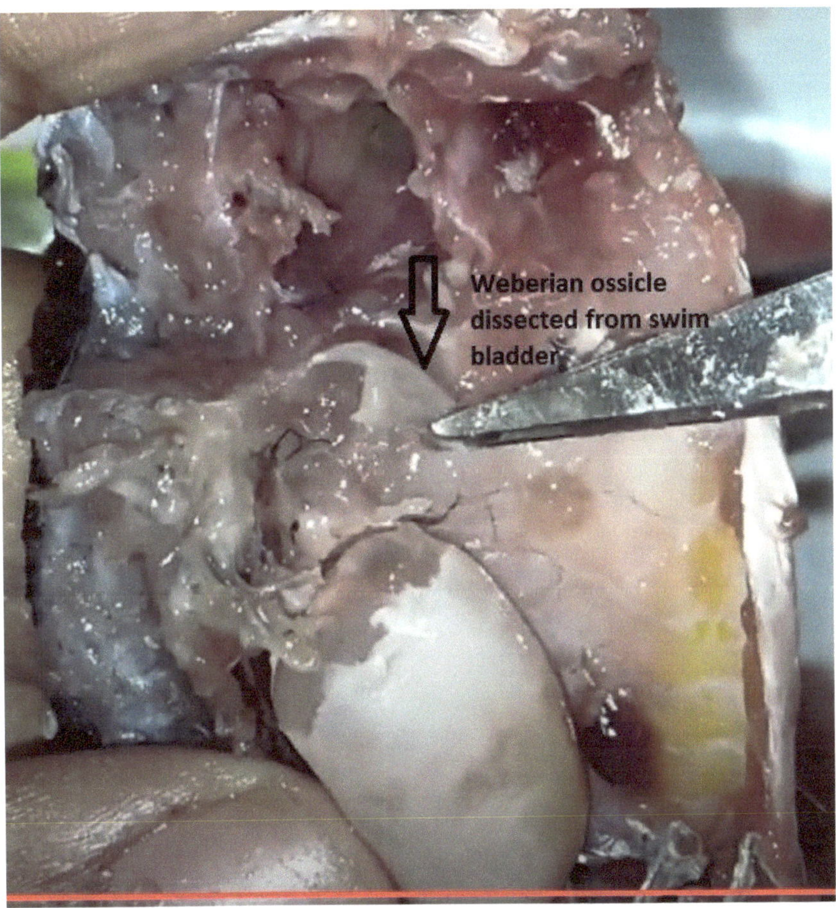

---

[24] This apparatus originates from the first few bones of the vertebrae, and grow to connect to the swim bladder acting like an inner ear.

be too tiny to be perceived by the inner ear structure alone.

The reason for these sounds or what they mean is yet to be determined.

Catfish, like carp, will come to the surface and gulp air if the diffused oxygen levels drop too low.

This unique ability to hear and make sounds may be related to the fact that some species can determine the *distance* of a sound's origin and its *direction*.

Swim Bladder

Most fish have a swim bladder. The swim bladder is filled with gas. It is merely an airbag organ in bony fish that enables them to control their **buoyancy** (and thus, depth). As mentioned above, it is also useful in communication. When the swim bladder expands with air, it will increase in volume and therefore displace more water. This increases the fish's buoyancy, and it will cause it to float upward. Removing the air causes it to sink. These properties were later used to create buoyancy vests used by scuba divers today.

The swim bladder is connected to the esophageal lining. In some fish, the gas inside the swim bladder is obtained by gulping surface air. In other fish, the swim bladder is filled under pressure with gases, mainly oxygen, which diffused from the blood and actions of the gas gland.

Hibernation?

Catfish do not **hibernate** in winter. But catfish do behave differently in winter than in summer. The temperature has

an effect. Fish are **poikilothermic**. This means that their internal temperature varies considerably.[25] Body temperature is critical for the proper **metabolic** function of *enzymes* and *catalysts*. Also, extremely warm temperatures can, besides limiting diffused oxygen content, **denature** proteins. Once denatured, they are destroyed and costly to replenish.

---

[25] It is the opposite of a homeotherm, an animal that maintains thermal homeostasis because its liver generates enough heat to maintain a temperature range.

Catfish, and all fish, are cold-blooded and have to regulate their body temperature as their livers provide little heat. Unlike reptiles (turtles or alligators), fish cannot climb up on land to bask in the sun.[26] However, they can move up and down the thermocline to warmer or colder zones. Moving to warmer or colder zones enables them to have some control over body temperature.

As a result, most fish are less active during colder water temperatures. During winters, the catfish's metabolism may slow, causing them to become less vigorous, but the fish still have to eat. The big fish have to eat more often. That still requires them to hunt and secure food during cold seasons. Winter catfish often are found resting in large holes (not necessarily deep) with slow-moving water. As the season progresses and water temperatures warm from longer days and more direct sunlight, the catfish can be found moving more up and downstream from their winter nests.

Reproduction

Catfish are **monogamous**, meaning they have only one mate during the **spawning** season. Most major catfish species **spawn** during spring or summer when the water warms to an optimal temperature.[27] Salinity affects not only fish and their bodies but also their eggs.

Adult male catfish are responsible for preparing a **nest**,

---

[26] There are a few species that actually do leave the water and throws themselves on shore. The mangrove rivulus fish (Kryptolebias *marmoratus*) flings itself onto land when the water gets too hot. This is called *evaporative cooling*. As the fish's wet skin dries, its body temperature drops (cools). Once cooled off it flips and flops its way back into the water.
[27] Channel and blue catfish spawn at 70-84ºF (21.1-28.9ºC), but 80-81ºF (26.7ºC-27.2ºC) is considered best by some. Flatheads spawn at 66-75ºF (18.9ºC-23.9ºC).

which can be deep or shallow and often just a hole or depressed area on the lake's bottom or stream. Nests are also created in secluded undercut banks and burrows. Channel catfish are *cavity nesters*, meaning they lay their eggs in crevices. The sticky egg mass is deposited there by the female.

Under commercial fish farming conditions, males can fertilize as many as nine spawns a season. The male briefly guards the eggs and the young. Once the nest is established, a female will lay between 4,000 and 100,000 eggs, depending on the species. When the babies hatch, they stay in the nest for a week. Though the egg and minnow stage are the most vulnerable to death or predation, it appears that the adult survival rate is as high as 80 percent in some, like the channel catfish.

Within a week of egg-laying, so many eggs hatch that the baby catfishes (called **fries**) soon fill the nest. The mother will provide parental care and supervision and a steady supply of algae so that they can grow and mature. By the second week, they begin to leave the nest as a group, swarming together like bees around a hive. This behavior is called **shoaling** and helps in the catching and eating of small insects.

Shoaling is done for social purposes, whereas **schooling** moves in synchrony and unison in a coordinated manner. Swimming at the same speed and staying close together has the primary advantage of protection and hunting prey. Shoaling multiplies the number of eyes watching for danger and the directions in which they are looking for predators. Shoaling and schooling are different terms with different meanings but often are loosely used.

After two to three weeks, they are ready to venture out on their own. Most catfish are mature by the time they are 12 inches (30.5 cm) long. Catfish continue to grow with age. The larger the fish, the older it usually is. As a result, some humongous catfish have been caught in North American waters.

On average, channel catfish weigh between two to seven pounds and measure 12 to 24 inches long. However, many grow much larger than this, with the record weighing 58 pounds and measuring 52 inches. Catfish do have predators and are even preyed upon by other fish. Small channel catfish are especially hunted and preyed upon by flathead catfish and muskies. However, those who do reach a larger size seem to survive most predation. A catfish's average lifespan is about 15-20 years, with some reaching 40 to 60 years of age.

Miscellaneous

Fish do not sleep, at least not in the same way mammals sleep. Fish do rest, and they do so by reducing their activity and metabolism while remaining alert to potential danger. While some fish float in the resting state, others wedge themselves into some secure location in the mud or some suitable nest. One can recognize this resting state because the fish will be motionless, either at the bottom or near the water's surface. They are also slow to respond to stimuli going on around them or may not react at all. But by watching their gills, one can tell they are breathing slowly.

Some catfish are being recognized as potential **keystone species**. Losing them to the habitat in which they live would significantly alter life for other plants and animals. Keystone species are animals that become critical to a balanced ecosystem. For example, a beaver is a keystone species. The environment that it creates attracts and supports other wildlife but removing them would significantly change that environment and affect many other animals. A few environments where catfish are thriving have given indications that they, too, might become keystone species in that habitat. Besides, catfish, the bottom-dwellers, are an essential fish in North America, not only for sports fishing but also as a food source. Catching them can be quite a thrill, and frying them can be quite delectable and mouthwatering.

In North America, there are 54 species of native catfish, an important food source and a popular sporting fish. These include various species commonly called bullheads, madtoms, channel catfish, and blue catfish. Here we list some of the most common catfish species for the reader desiring to research any specific ones.

NORTH AMERICAN CATFISH

(orange or blue represents native; purple indicates non-native or introduced)

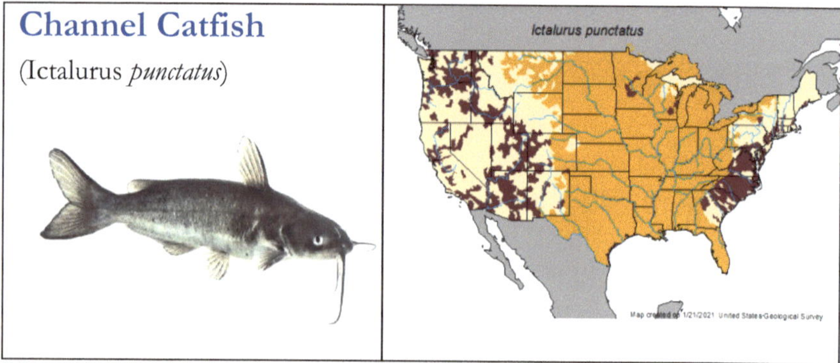

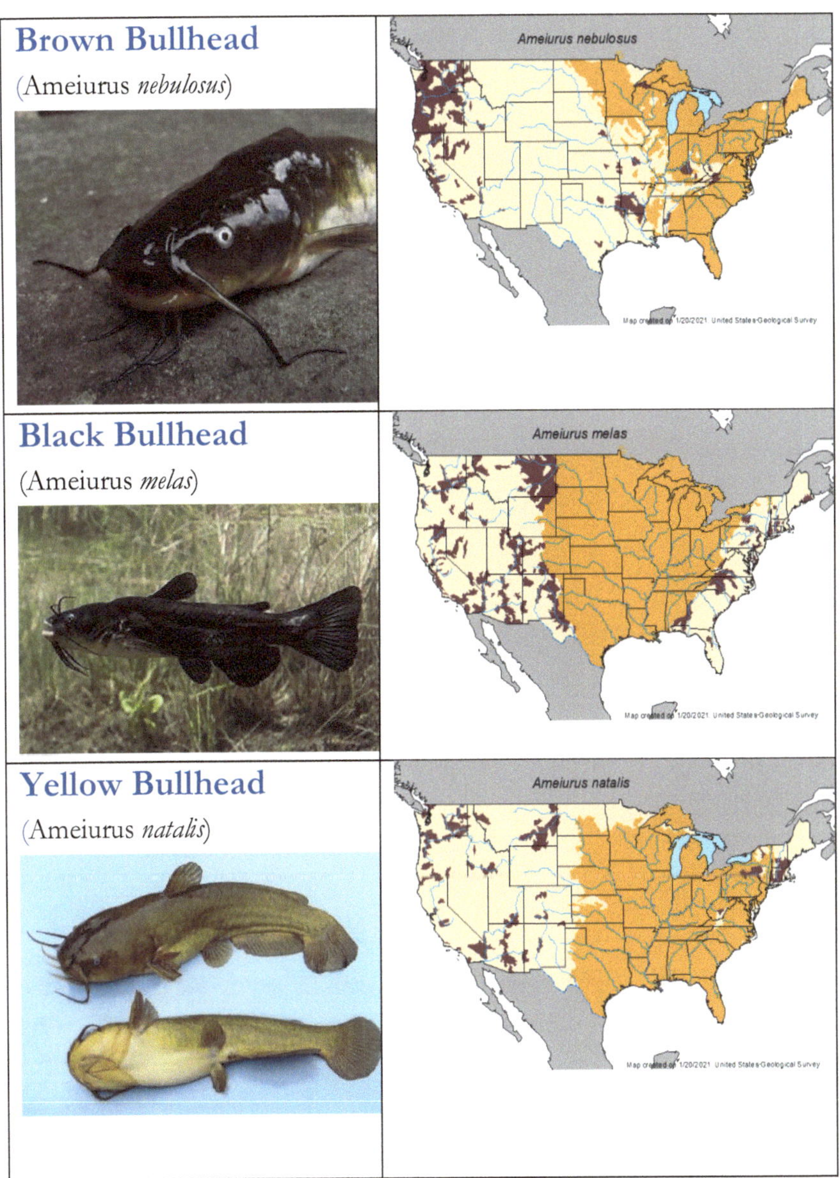

Brown Bullhead
(Ameiurus nebulosus)
Ameiurus nebulosus
Map created on 1/20/2021. United States Geological Survey
Black Bullhead
(Ameiurus melas)
Ameiurus melas
Map created on 1/20/2021. United States Geological Survey
Yellow Bullhead
(Ameiurus natalis)
Ameiurus natalis
Map created on 1/20/2021. United States Geological Survey

Flathead Catfish

(Pylodictis *olivaris*)

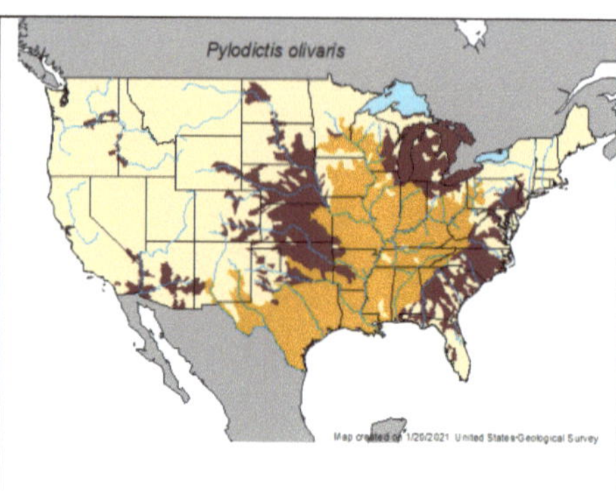

Blue Catfish

(Ictalurus *furcatus*)

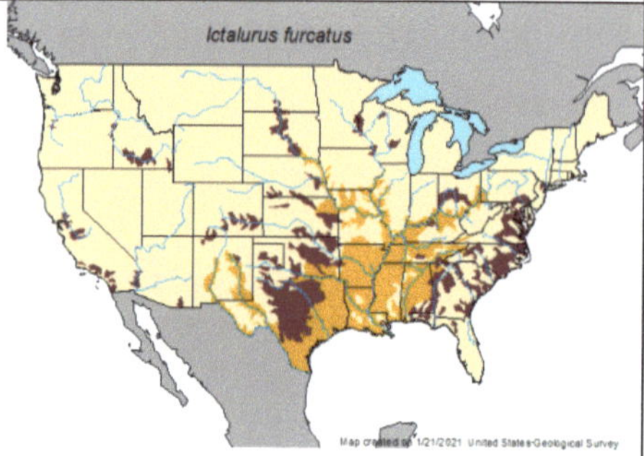

- The largest North American catfish species, reaching a length of 165 cm (65 in) and a weight of 68 kg (150 lbs.).

Stonecat Madtom

(Noturus *flavus*)

- *Occasionally are found in tiny creeks, or rivers as large as the Lower Mississippi, and in the northern Ozarks and northern half of Missouri.*

Map Unavailable

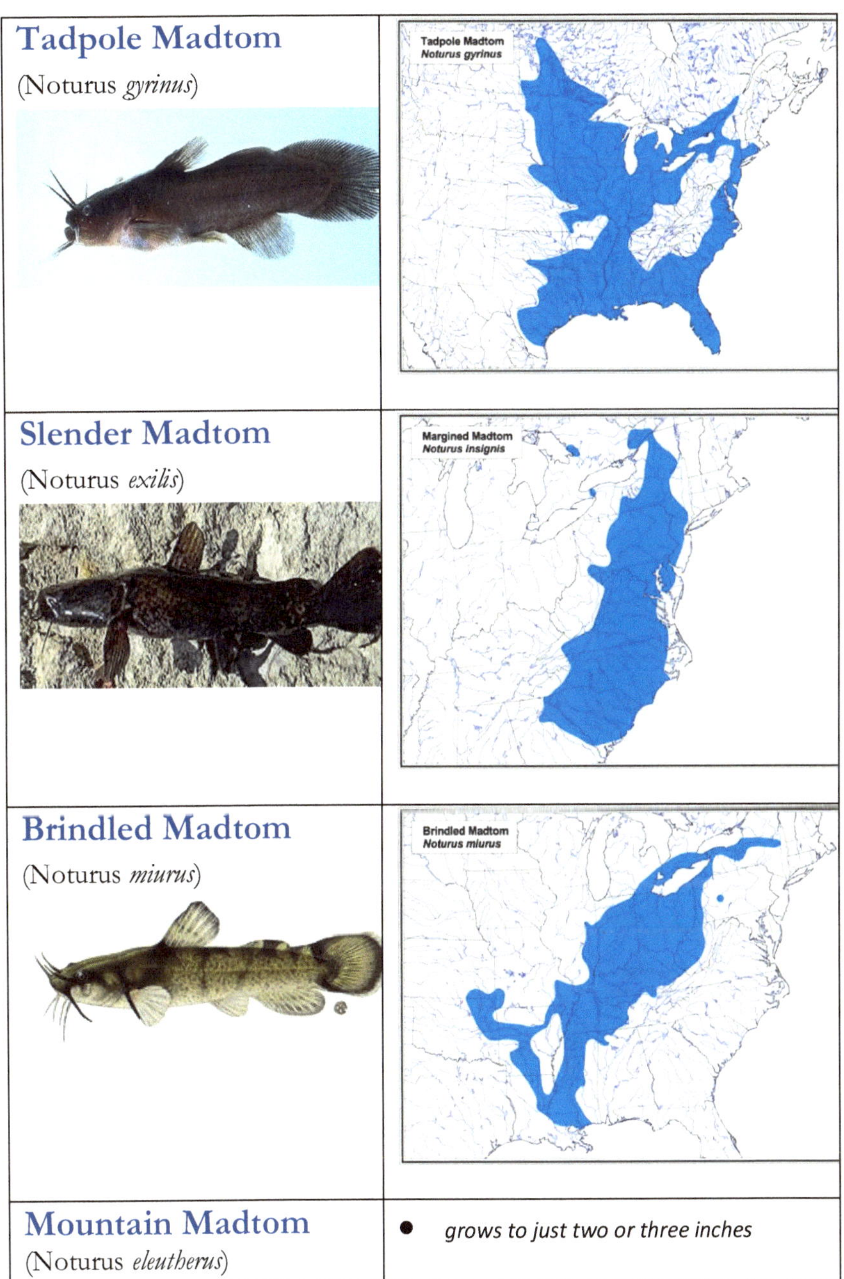

Tadpole Madtom

(Noturus *gyrinus*)

Slender Madtom

(Noturus *exilis*)

Brindled Madtom

(Noturus *miurus*)

Mountain Madtom
(Noturus *eleutherus*)

- *grows to just two or three inches*

Margined Madtom
(Noturus *insignis*)

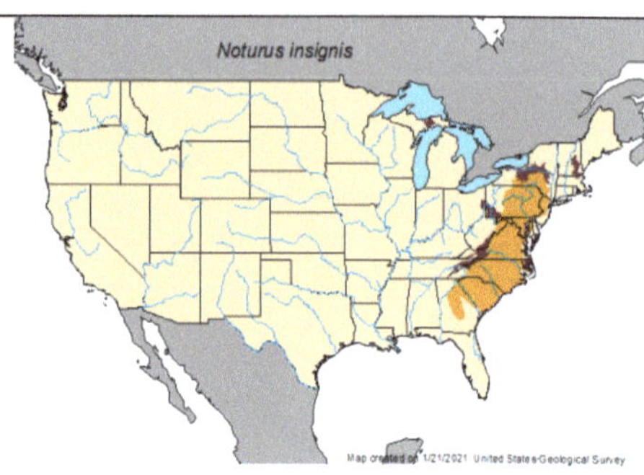

Gafftopsail catfish
(Bagre *marinus*)

- Found in the waters of the western central Atlantic Ocean, the Gulf of Mexico, and the Caribbean Sea.

Map Unavailable

Hardhead catfish
(Noturus *insignis*)

- Found mostly in the western Atlantic Ocean's near-shore waters, around the southeast coast of the United States, around the Florida Keys, and the coast of the Gulf of Mexico.

Map Unavailable

REVIEW

1. What class are fish considered taxonomically, and why were they given this name?

2. What are four characteristics of Osteichthyes?

3. Explain the difference between bottom dwellers and bottom feeders?

4. Do catfish communicate, and if so, how?

5. Though catfish do not hibernate, why might they seem to be in small numbers during winter?

6. What is newly hatched young catfish called, and how do they survive being so small?

7. What is the main factor catfish can become so large?

8. Which species of catfish tend to be the smallest?

9. Which species of catfish tend to be the largest?

10. How do catfish end up in ponds out in the middle of the woods?

CHANNEL CATFISH

COLORING PAGE

http://www.supercoloring.com/coloring-pages/channel-catfishes

Catfish: Bottom-Dwellers

Name:_______________________

Carefully read each statement or clue. Insert the correct letter into the box provided. Use the Word Bank if needed.

eggs   buoyancy   monogamous   Gafftopsail   poikilothermic   thermoclines   schooling

Weberian   schoaling   cones   gulp   lifespan   spawn   bone   rods   Osteichthyes

Across

4. _______ average for catfish is about 15-20 years,

6. Cells that provides night vision?

7. Fishing moving in harmony and synchronized?

9. One of the marine catfish?

10. Most catfish regulate their body temperature by changing _______.

12. What taxonomic class are fish in?

14. Cells that provide color vision?

16. Swim bladder provides fish was _______-

Down

1. osteo- means

2. Fishing staying together for social or safety reasons?

3. During mating seasons most catfish tend to stay with one mate.

5. Fish are cold-blooded.

8. 4,000 to 100,000 tends to be the number of _______ spawned.

11. Clicking noises heard in the water might be the result of the _______ ossicles.

13. To lay eggs.

15. If diffused oxygen drops too low, fish often come to the surface and _______.

INTERESTING SOURCES TO CONSIDER

Adult Channel Catfish Guarding Fry Inside Spawning Box at Lake Marburg. Available at: https://youtu.be/GpiJR8ZfA34

Catfish and Carp: The catfish is known by many different local names. Available at: https://youtu.be/ZGqzUE7YgHY

Catfish spawning and hatching. Available at: https://youtu.be/k24GZdcXNiY

Channel Catfish Breeding in Sunken Tire. Available at: https://youtu.be/-ZVZWSVHJaI

Face to Face: Blue Catfish. Available at: https://youtu.be/iag4EjVUrow

Fish Species in North America: Underwater Minute. Available at: https://youtu.be/cUgw93waVyM

How to identify catfish - flathead, blue, channel, white catfish, bullhead and other species. Available at: https://youtu.be/ks1X6NnvfhA

Huge blue catfish. Available at: https://youtu.be/rcoc7Qe2qYU

Interesting facts about Blue catfish by weird square. Available at: https://youtu.be/ij8b42DJLKw

Invasive Species: 10 Species Invading North America (2018). Available at: https://youtu.be/G1hJ-NmO8hE

Largest Catfish ever caught on film in North America. Available at: https://youtu.be/80BUfQgBap4

Male Channel Catfish, 4 yrs 9 mos old, nesting box. Available at: https://youtu.be/tgKR2VO9Ny4

Native Catfish Farming: Inside the most successful catfish farm. Available at: https://youtu.be/b36FArmZ8M4

North American Fishing Club: Monster Catfish Part 5 Channel Catfish. Available at: https://youtu.be/Dgq_zk1TThE

North American Flathead Catfish Skull. Pylodictis *olivaris*. Available at: https://youtu.be/uBjud39VLvU

Placing spawning cans for channel catfish. Available at: https://youtu.be/JpCvsTyP6BA

The "Big Three" Types of Catfish (and How to Identify Them): Catfish Species Essentials. Available at: https://youtu.be/9nrzv8KT8s4

ABOUT THE AUTHOR

Richard NeSmith is a native of Florida, USA. He grew up wading through the swamps of central Florida with his two younger brothers during the pre-Disney era, and unknowingly, falling in love with biology, wildlife, and nature. He has lived in seven American states, twice in Australia and once in Mexico City. He holds eight university degrees and has taught for 14 years in secondary schools, here and abroad, and another 13 years as a professor in several American universities. His service includes professor of science education, Dean of Education, Campus Dean, as well as an online instructor. His passion for learning (and *how we learn*) did not develop until *after* graduating from high school. His only explanation for this is that *having a goal made all the difference in the world*. He enjoys reading, hiking, nature photography, golf, tennis, and RV camping.

http://richardnesmith.obior.cc

Applied Principles of Education & Learning *presents*

APE-Learning

AMAZON AUTHOR's PAGE:

https://www.amazon.com/author/richardnesmith

Educational, wildlife, and naturalist books
Dr. Richard NeSmith.

Issue 1
Raccoons:
Friendly Bandits
Dr. Richard NeSmith

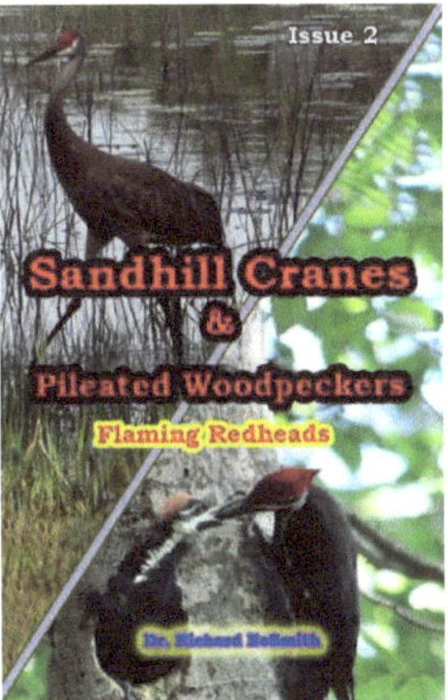
Issue 2
Sandhill Cranes
&
Pileated Woodpeckers
Flaming Redheads
Dr. Richard NeSmith

Issue 3
American
Alligators
&
Crocodiles
Dr. Richard NeSmith

Issue 4
Bobcats:
Ghostly Elusive
Dr. Richard NeSmith

Issue 5
Foxes:
Sneaky Rascals
Dr. Richard NeSmith

Issue 6
Armadillo:
Little Armored One
Dr. Richard NeSmith

Issue 7
Squirrels:
Bushy Tail Scampers
Dr. Richard NeSmith

Issue 8
River Otters:
Aquatic Clowns !
Dr. Richard NeSmith

Issue 9
Beavers:
Nature's Engineers !
Dr. Richard NeSmith

Issue 10
Black Bears
Titans of the Forest
Dr. Richard NeSmith

Issue 11
Freshwater
Turtles
Dr. Richard NeSmith

Issue 12
FUNGI, LICHENS
& MUSHROOMS
Dr. Richard NeSmith

Paperbacks: http://amazon.com/author/richardnesmith

e-books: https://bit.ly/3iuCgB3

---

[i] **Special thanks to the following who kindly provided permission to use their photographs.**

From Unsplash: Will Turner.

From Pixabay: David Mark, Deedster, Pexels, Alison Cave, Jakob Owensand, and Filip Kalaj.

Finally, *special thanks* to likeminded friends who love wildlife and who willingly shared their wonderful photos, and many of whom have become my friends: **Fédération de pêche, Michael Gardner, Greg Jowers** and various government **federal and state wildlife divisions**.

If you enjoyed this book, please go to amazon.com and share a nice review. 

Thank you everyone.

Love Learning – Love Nature – Love Life

54